Now You're COOKING

HEALTHY RECIPES FROM
LATIN AMERICA

MEXICO

Tamra Orr

PURPLE TOAD
PUBLISHING

P.O. Box 631
Kennett Square, Pennsylvania 19348
www.purpletoadpublishing.com

Now You're COOKING

HEALTHY RECIPES FROM
LATIN AMERICA

Brazil

Cuba

Guatemala

Mexico

Puerto Rico

PUBLISHER'S NOTE: The data in this book has been researched in depth, and to the best of our knowledge is factual. Although every measure is taken to give an accurate account, Purple Toad Publishing makes no warranty of the accuracy of the information and is not liable for damages caused by inaccuracies.

Printing   1   2   3   4   5   6   7   8   9

Publisher's Cataloging-in-Publication Data
Orr, Tamra
    Now You Are Cooking: Mexico / Tamra Orr
      p. cm.—(Now you're cooking. Healthy recipes from Latin America)
Includes bibliographic references and index.
ISBN: 978-1-62469-036-5 (library bound)
1. Cooking, Mexican. 2. Cooking—Juvenile literature. 3. Recipes for health.   I. Title.
 TX716.M4 2013
 641.5972—dc23
                                    2013936071

eBook ISBN: 9781624690372

Printed by Lake Book Manufacturing, Chicago, IL

CONTENTS

Introduction

Welcome to Mexico!

What is six feet long, two feet wide, takes up to 12 hours to cook and can feed more than 50 people?

If you answered a fabulous Mexican tamale called a *zacahuil,* you are absolutely right! Zacahuil means "big bite" and it is a tradition in the Huasteca region of Mexico.

Have you ever tasted a tamale? It is a delicious dish that comes wrapped in banana leaves and stuffed full of meat, rice, beans, and salsa. If you happen to be walking through the Huasteca region some weekend, you would not only get the chance to nibble on this tasty treat, but marvel at its size! These special tamales are huge! The ingredients change from one part of the region to the next. While one might include seafood, the next might use shredded chicken. One might be mild whereas another might be full of spicy hot peppers. Tamales are only one of the wonderful dishes that are found in this exciting country.

Mexico and the United States are geographic neighbors that are both part of the continent of North America. The states of California, Arizona, New Mexico and Texas all have borders with Mexico. Because of its Spanish heritage, Mexico is also considered to be in Latin America. Mexico is three times the size of Texas and is home to over 112 million people.

Giant tamales like this are a popular tradition in the Huasteca region of Mexico.

While many people think of pyramids only being in Egypt, these amazing structures are found in Mexico's Teotihuacan region.

Long ago this land belonged to the Mayans and the Aztecs. When Spain invaded in the early 16th century, they introduced new animals, new foods and new ways of life to the people living there.

Mexico is a wonderful place for many reasons. Its national sport is bullfighting; it is part of the world's famous Ring of Fire, an area of violent earthquakes and volcanoes, and it is the place where millions of monarch butterflies go every winter to enjoy the sunny weather. Mexico is home to holidays such as Cinco de Mayo and Day of the Dead. Perhaps one of the most fascinating things about Mexico is its food! After all, this is the country that introduced chocolate to the rest of the world.

Mexican food is often spicy, and always full of flavor. The majority of it is made up of a combination of tortillas, rice, beans, meat and sauce. The shape, size, and mix of these ingredients create dishes, such as *tostadas, burritos, chalupas, quesadillas, tacos, chimichangas*, and *enchiladas*. Ready to learn more about them? Let's go!

Ceviche

Many of the meals found in Mexico start off with a bowl of soup. Some of these soups are thin, light broths full of flavor and herbs. Others are thick and rich, with huge chunks that call more for a fork than a spoon! Cream is rarely used to thicken the soups. Instead, Latin American cooks use potatoes, nuts and seeds to create a heartier dish. In addition, Mexicans often add flavor and texture to their soups by adding strips of fried tortillas or a healthy spoonful of sour cream.

Ceviche (seh-VEE-chay) is a soup that is popular throughout all of Latin America, including Mexico. It is very light, and refreshing soup. It is often eaten as a snack or before the main dish at lunch. Ceviche dates back many years. Because this soup is not actually cooked, it was a favorite of the Inca, especially after the Spanish conquistadors came to the area and added lime to the mix. Soaking the fish in the sour lime and lemon juices changes the consistency of the fish. It makes it firmer, as if it has been cooked. Because of the risks associated with eating uncooked or under-cooked fish, we recommend cooking the fish first.

This light soup can be made with a variety of different types of fish, including salmon, mackerel, bass, shrimp, or scallops. If you had a bowl of it in Chile, it would have grapefruit juice and cilantro added, whereas in Peru it would have slices of onion. In Mexico, it is often served alongside boiled white or sweet potatoes or hot corn on the cob.

Ingredients

1   pound halibut or other firm white fish fillets
     juice of 3 limes
     juice of 2 lemons
2   red chile peppers
     salt to taste

Ceviche

¼ cup orange juice
3 tomatoes, peeled, seeded, and finely diced
3 tablespoons vegetable oil
3 tablespoons coarsely chopped fresh cilantro leaves
2 scallions, white and green parts, finely chopped
 pinch cayenne pepper
1 ripe avocado, peeled, pitted, and diced
 freshly-ground black pepper to taste

Directions

1. Cut the fish into 1 ½-inch chunks.
2. Combine the fish, lime and lemon juices, the chilies, and salt; toss well.
3. Cover and refrigerate for two hours, stirring occasionally.
4. Add the remaining ingredients and toss gently to blend the flavors.

Sweet Potato, Corn, and Green Chili Soup

Another popular soup option that is sure to fill up your stomach is one made with chunks of sweet potatoes, corn and lightly spicy green chilies. Both of these starches—potatoes and corn— are favorites in Mexican cooking. Sweet potatoes are used in a wide variety of ways, from soups and side dishes to main dishes, salads and desserts. Even the skins are used as a dish! Many Mexican cooks take the skins and fill them with roasted corn, black beans, some spicy sauce, and a little melted cheese. Tasty!

Experts have found sweet potato dishes used all the way back to the time of the Maya. This recipe for a thick soup is delicious when paired with bread or tortillas.

Ingredients

¼   cup butter
1   medium onion, finely chopped
1¾ cups sweet potatoes, (about 5 medium potatoes), peeled and chopped
4   cups chicken stock
2   cups fresh or frozen sweet corn
1   Fresno or jalapeño chili pepper, seeded and finely diced*
     salt and freshly-ground black pepper

Directions

1. Have **an adult** melt the butter in a large saucepan over medium-high heat.
2. Add the onion; cook and stir until tender, about 5 minutes.
3. Add the sweet potatoes and stock and bring to a boil. Reduce the heat to low.
4. Cover and simmer until the potatoes are tender, about 20 minutes
5. Strain the soup, and place the solids and liquids separately.

Sweet potato, corn, and
green chili soup

6. Place the solids in a blender or food processer and blend until smooth.
7. Return the stock to the rinsed-out pan and add the potato puree.
8. Add the corn and chili pepper. Season with the salt and pepper to taste.
9. Simmer an additional 10 minutes. If the soup is too thick, add additional chicken stock and simmer until thoroughly heated.

*NOTE: Be sure to wear plastic gloves when you handle hot peppers. The seeds and pulp on the inside of the peppers can irritate your skin! And never touch your eyes or face with the gloves after you have touched the pepper seeds.

Two-Bean Chili with Vegetables

When you think about Mexican food, you may immediately think of big, bubbling pots of chili. People have often thought that chili was originally invented somewhere in Mexico since it uses many of the same ingredients that it is known for, but the truth is, chili started in 17th century Spain. It is not commonly offered in Mexico, and seldom found in local restaurants, but when it is prepared, it is delicious. Here is one of the main ways of preparing this spicy dish. It can be put into deep stew bowls, served over piles of rice or potatoes, or even added to omelets, or as filling for tortillas.

Ingredients

2   tablespoons vegetable oil
2   large onions, chopped
4   garlic cloves, crushed
1½ pounds ground chicken
2   teaspoons mild chili powder
2   teaspoons ground cumin
½   teaspoon cayenne pepper
2   cans (14 ½ ounces each) diced tomatoes, un-drained
2½ cups beef stock
2   medium potatoes, peeled and cut into1-inch cubes
1   large carrot, peeled and cut into 1-inch pieces
2   celery stalks, diced
1   red bell pepper, seeded and diced
1   can (15 ounces) red kidney beans, drained and rinsed
1   can (15 ounces) pinto beans, drained and rinsed
     salt and freshly-ground pepper to taste
½   teaspoon chili sauce

Two-bean chili

Directions

1. Have **an adult** heat the oil in a covered metal casserole pot. Add the onions and cook over very low heat until almost tender, about 10 minutes.
2. Add the garlic and ground beef and cook, stirring constantly with a fork to break up meat.
3. Stir in the chili powder, cumin, and cayenne and cook for three minutes
4. Mix in the tomatoes, stock, potatoes, carrot, celery, and bell pepper and bring to a boil.
5. Reduce the heat, cover and simmer for 40 minutes.
6. Stir in the beans, season to taste with salt, pepper, and chili sauce and continue simmering for 15 minutes, or until all the flavors are well blended.

Garlic-Roasted Chicken

with Sweet Potatoes

Long ago, when the 18 countries that make up Latin America were developing, people ate things that are now considered inedible: dogs, lizards, rabbits, and some insects.

Even today, traditional dishes can include snake, armadillo, monkeys and even giant ant eggs!

Here are some main dish recipes that use chicken and seafood instead. They are healthier, safer, and more to our taste today!

Ingredients

1   (4-pound) roasting chicken
4   tablespoons chicken stock
6   garlic cloves, crushed
    juice of 2 lemons
2   tablespoons butter, melted
1   green apple, cored and quartered
    salt and freshly-ground pepper to taste
2   tablespoons chopped fresh parsley
1   teaspoon chopped fresh thyme leaves
1½ pounds sweet potatoes, peeled and cut into rounds 1 inch thick
2   medium onions, thinly sliced
2   tablespoons olive oil

Directions

1. Have **an adult** wipe the chicken inside and out with a damp paper towel.
2. In a small bowl, mix together the stock, half of the garlic, the lemon juice and melted butter; brush it all over the chicken.
3. Place the apple quarters inside the breast cavity of the chicken.
4. Season with salt and pepper, then place in an ovenproof casserole dish with a tight-fitting lid.

chicken with sweet
potatoes

5. In a small bowl, mix together the parsley and thyme.
6. Arrange layers of sweet potatoes, onions, and the remaining garlic around the chicken, scattering the herbs evenly over each layer.
7. Season with additional salt and pepper. Drizzle the sweet potatoes with olive oil.
8. Cover the casserole dish tightly and place the chicken in a cold oven. Bake at 400° F for one hour.
9. Check that the potatoes are not getting too dry. If they are, drizzle them with a few tablespoons of chicken stock.
10. Continue baking, covered, for an additional 30 minutes.
11. Remove the lid from the casserole dish and bake an additional 15 minutes or until the inside of the chicken registers 165° F on a meat thermometer and is no longer pink in the center, and the sweet potatoes are slightly browned.
12. Serve hot with rice.

Salmon Tacos

Latin America has thousands of miles of coastline, so it can access an incredible variety of fish and seafood! Shellfish like lobsters, crab, and shrimp are popular. The more tropical areas of Latin America rely on dolphin fish, and mahi for special occasions, and cod, grouper, and sardines for daily meals.

Fish is used in many different recipes, and salmon is a favorite throughout Mexico. In this recipe, it is added to tacos. Tacos can be made with corn or flower tortillas, have have either soft or hard shells, and can have many different fillings and toppings. Try this one topped with salsa and guacamole! It uses the grill and has a sweet marinade for extra flavor.

Main Ingredients

4 (6-ounce) salmon fillets, skinned
1 can (14 ounces) black beans, drained and rinsed
2 tablespoons chopped fresh cilantro leaves
2 tablespoons vegetable oil
  juice of 1 lime

Ingredients for the marinade

¾ cup honey
2 tablespoons coarse-grained brown mustard
  juice of 1 lemon
2 teaspoons ground cumin
1 teaspoon ground cilantro
1 teaspoon chili powder
  salt and freshly-ground black pepper

Directions

1. In a large shallow dish, combine all of the marinade ingredients. Mix well.

Salmon tacos

2. Coat salmon with marinade. Cover and refrigerate up to one hour.
3. Have **an adult** heat the grill on high.
4. Place the salmon on a baking sheet and grill without turning until fish flakes easily with a fork.
5. Remove from the grill; cover to keep warm.
6. Preheat the oven to 350° F.
7. Wrap the tortillas in aluminum foil, place in the oven, and heat until warmed, about 10 minutes. You can also place a stack of the shells in the microwave for under a minute.
8. In a medium bowl, mix together the black beans, cilantro, oil, and lime juice, season with salt and pepper to taste.
9. Arrange the grilled salmon, lettuce, bean mixture, and lime wedges on a large platter.

Root Vegetable Gratin

Vegetables, or *verduras,* are an essential part of the Mexican menu. Root vegetables, such as potatoes, are used most often. In some parts of Latin America, there are more than 100 different types of potatoes! They come in many different sizes and shapes. They even range in color from black to bright orange.

During the late 1800s and early 1900s, immigrants from many different countries came to Mexico and other parts of Latin America. Naturally, they brought their own types of food with them, greatly increasing the number of vegetables found in Mexico today. This recipe puts sweet potatoes to good use and makes a terrific side dish that resembles the French dish Potatoes au Gratin.

Ingredients
¾ pound sweet potatoes, peeled and shredded
¾ pound celery root, peeled and shredded
¾ pound turnips, peeled and shredded
1¼ cups heavy cream
½ teaspoon cayenne pepper
 salt and freshly-ground pepper
2 tablespoons shredded Cheddar cheese
1 tablespoon dry white bread crumbs

Directions
1. Have **an adult** preheat the oven to 400° F
2. In a large bowl, combine the shredded vegetables, cream, and cayenne. Season with salt and pepper.
3. Spoon the mixture into a greased shallow dish.
4. Cover tightly with foil and bake for about 30 minutes or until the vegetables are cooked.
5. Remove the mixture from the oven.
6. Have **an adult** heat the broiler.

Root vegetable gratin

7. Combine the cheese and bread crumbs; sprinkle evenly over the mix.
8. Broil, uncovered, until the cheese is brown and bubbly. Serve at once.

Shredded Kale

If you have never had kale, or *col rizada* as it is known in Mexico, you aren't alone. Kale is found in most American grocery stores, but most people are not sure what to do with it other than add it to salads, so you may not have had it in a recipe. In Mexico, many farmers' markets have several kinds of kale and it is typically inexpensive, so a popular choice. Here is one way to make it. As you try a serving, remember that there is a reason kale is sometimes referred to as the "queen of greens." It is low in calories, and high in fiber. It is bursting with vitamins A, C and K. Doctors often recommend kale as one of the superfoods to eat to lower the risk of obesity, heart disease, and cancer. Maybe you should have a second helping!

Ingredients

2   pounds kale or collard greens
3   tablespoons vegetable oil
1   garlic clove, crushed
          salt and freshly-ground pepper
          juice of ½ lime

Directions

1. Wash the kale thoroughly. Have **an adult** cut the leaves from their tough stems.
2. Stack several leaves at a time on top of each other, roll up and have **an adult** cut crosswise into thin slices to shred finely.
3. Have **an adult** heat the oil in a large sauté pan over low heat.
4. Add the garlic and cook for one minute.
5. Increase the heat to medium, and add the shredded kale. Stir for one minute.
6. Cover and cook for 5 to 8 minutes or until wilted.
7. Remove the lid, turn the heat to high and boil for two minutes or until all the liquid is gone.
8. Season to taste with salt and pepper and add the lime juice.
9. Serve hot or cold.

Shredded kale
in a pan

Elote
(Mexican Corn on the Cob)

Corn is a vegetable that is popular throughout all parts of Latin America. It is often added to salsas and salads, included in burritos and tacos, or just eaten by itself. Corn on the cob is often sold by street vendors as the perfect afternoon snack. Try adding these toppings to transform corn on the cob into something special!

Ingredients

4   ears of corn
¼   cup melted butter
¼   cup light mayonnaise
½   cup grated Cotija cheese
4   wedges of lime
   cayenne pepper (optional)

Directions

1. Cook the corn cobs by having **an adult** put them into a pot of boiling water for 6 to 8 minutes.
2. Carefully handle the hot corn! Roll the cob in melted butter.
3. Apply a light layer of mayonnaise.
4. Sprinkle with grated Cotija cheese (a goat's milk cheese that originates in Mexico.)
5. Squirt lime juice over the whole cob.
6. If you like a little spice, add sprinkles of cayenne pepper.

What a way to eat your vegetables!

Elote

Tortillas, Frijoles, Arroz y Mas
(Tortillas, Beans, Rice, and More)

Some bean fields in Mexico are still ploughed by patient farmers with mules.

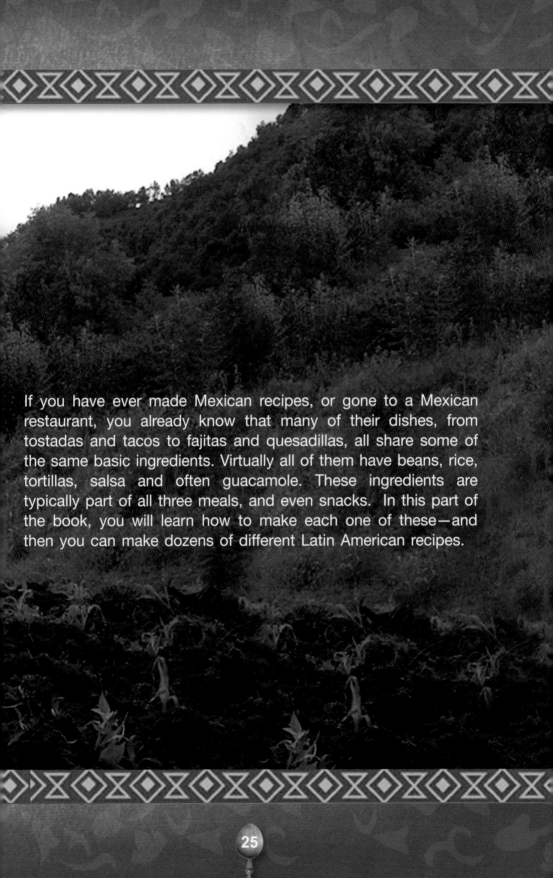

If you have ever made Mexican recipes, or gone to a Mexican restaurant, you already know that many of their dishes, from tostadas and tacos to fajitas and quesadillas, all share some of the same basic ingredients. Virtually all of them have beans, rice, tortillas, salsa and often guacamole. These ingredients are typically part of all three meals, and even snacks. In this part of the book, you will learn how to make each one of these—and then you can make dozens of different Latin American recipes.

Milky Coconut Beans

Beans, or *frijoles*, may sound dull, but when it comes to Mexican food—they aren't! Mexicans use a wide variety of beans, including black, kidney, pinto, and lima. They mash them, fry them, and boil them, and add exotic blends of spices to enhance the flavors. Here is a recipe for an unusual but delicious blend of bean and coconut.

Ingredients

8 ounces dried black beans
1 14-ounce can thick coconut milk
½ teaspoon cayenne pepper
½ teaspoon granulated sugar
1 teaspoon salt

Directions

1. Place the beans in a large sauce pan or bowl. Add enough water to cover and soak the beans overnight, then cook according to the instructions on the package.
2. Drain the beans and discard the cooking water. Put the beans and the coconut milk in a blender. Blend until smooth and creamy.
3. Place the mixture in a large saucepan. Add the cayenne pepper, sugar, and salt and bring to a boil. (If the mixture is too thick, add a few tablespoons of water. If it is too thin, boil the mixture longer. It should be about as thick as mashed potatoes.)
4. Serve warm.

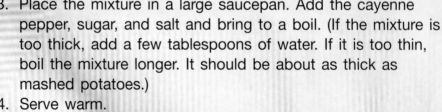

Coconut and black beans

Mexican Rice

Rice, or *arroz,* did not originally come from Mexico, but from China. It was brought to the area in the 16th century by the Spanish and was an immediate hit. When rice is combined with beans, it creates what is known as a "complete" protein, an essential part of a healthy diet. Throughout Mexico, rice is added to soups and usually combined with tortillas and beans.

Here is a simple recipe for basic rice. Some variations include adding the golden spice turmeric to make yellow rice, or emerald-colored parsley and cilantro to make green rice. Some cooks include raisins and walnuts to create chunkier, sweeter rice, or add additional chopped vegetables, such as zucchini, chile or bell peppers.

Ingredients

1	cup plus 2 tablespoons uncooked long-grain white rice
3	medium tomatoes, halved
1	medium onion, halved
2	garlic cloves, crushed
4	tablespoons vegetable oil
	salt and freshly-ground black pepper
1¾	cup hot chicken stock
2	carrots, peeled and finely diced
¾	cup frozen peas, thawed
1	green chili, seeded and finely diced
½	red bell pepper, seeded and finely diced

Directions

1. Have **an adult** heat the grill to high.
2. Wash the rice in several changes of water and let it soak for 15 minutes. Drain thoroughly.

Mexican rice

3. Place the tomatoes, onion, and garlic on a baking sheet.
4. Drizzle with two tablespoons of oil and season with salt and pepper. Grill, stirring occasionally, until the tomatoes and onions are lightly browned, about 10 minutes.
5. Transfer the grilled vegetable mixture to a blender or food processor and blend until smooth. If too thick, add a few tablespoons of chicken stock.
6. Heat the remaining two tablespoons of oil in a large, heavy saucepan over medium-high heat.
7. Add the rice and cook, stirring constantly, until the rice is lightly golden but not burned, about 5 minutes.
8. Add the drained vegetable mixture and cook 5 more minutes
9. Stir in the carrots, peas, chili, red pepper, and chicken stock.
10. Season with salt and pepper.
11. Bring to a boil. Reduce the heat to low, cover, and simmer until the rice is tender and the liquid absorbed, about 20 minutes.

Have you ever thought about how often you eat a slice of bread? You might have some toast for breakfast, a sandwich for lunch, and then a slice of garlic bread with spaghetti for dinner. In Mexico, it is similar, except that they use corn or flour tortillas with most of their meals. Just like you can add a huge variety of toppings to bread—peanut butter, eggs, sliced meat, butter, cheese, or tomatoes, Mexicans also add toppings to their tortillas, including sliced meats, grated cheese, fresh salsas, chopped vegetables, and sprinkled cayenne or chili pepper.

Until the Spaniards brought wheat to Latin America, Mexicans relied on corn to make their flat breads. Now flour tortillas are just as popular. Here is how to make your own.

Ingredients

1¼ cups all-purpose whole wheat flour
1   teaspoon salt
¼   cup shortening
¾   cup warm water
1   teaspoon vegetable oil

Directions

1. Sift the flour and salt into a medium bowl.
2. Add the shortening.
3. Stir in enough water to form a soft but not sticky dough.
4. Knead the dough well on a floured surface for about 10 minutes or until smooth and elastic.
5. Put the dough into a clean bowl, cover, and set aside to rest for one hour.

Flour tortillas

6. Divide the dough into 13 equal pieces. Roll each piece on a lightly floured surface until about 8 inches wide.
7. Have **an adult** cook the tortillas one at a time in a heated skillet until the bottom has brown areas and bubbles develop on the top.
8. Turn the tortilla and cook the other side. Grease the pan very lightly with the oil only if the tortilla is sticking.
9. Keep the tortillas warm by wrapping them in a clean cloth until you are ready to use them.

Salsa Cruda

The word *salsa* literally means sauce, and that is exactly how it is used. Although salsa tends to vary from one cook to the next, some qualities stay the same. It is always made fresh (never more than two hours before it is going to be served), and it is served at room temperature. Salsa is put on top of tortillas, beans, rice, meat and vegetables. It is a dip for tortilla chips and a dressing for salad. When fruit is added to it, the salsa is put on barbequed meats. This recipe is for what is known as "table salsa" because it is very basic.

Ingredients

6   medium tomatoes, seeded and finely diced
1   medium red onion, finely chopped
2   scallions, white and green parts, coarsely chopped
2   tablespoons finely chopped fresh cilantro leaves
1   green Dutch or Westland chili, seeded and finely chopped
½   teaspoon finely chopped fresh oregano
    pinch of sugar
    juice of 1 lime or 2 lemons
3   tablespoons vegetable oil
    salt and freshly-ground black pepper

Directions

1. Combine all ingredients except the salt and black pepper in a medium bowl.
2. Mix well.
3. Season to taste with the salt and pepper.
4. Serve at room temperature.

Salsa is a topping that goes with almost
every Mexican dish put on the table.

Another common topping for many different Mexican dishes is guacamole (gwak-uh-MOH-lay). It is made out of ripe avocados and is used for a chip dip or to put on top of any number of tortilla dishes. Guacamole is a very old dish, dating back to the days of the Aztecs who were known for making an avocado mixture. When Mexicans make the dish, they often place the pit on the top of the sauce, in the belief that it will stop the dish from turning brown.

This recipe is for basic guacamole. To make it spicy add hot sauce or Jalapeño peppers. Try it with a pile of corn chips and a bowl of the salsa you just made.

Ingredients
2   very ripe avocados
    juice of 1 lime
1   small onion, finely chopped
1   teaspoon salt
    boiling water
2   medium tomatoes, seeded and chopped
2   red jalapeño peppers, finely chopped (optional) *
    dash of hot sauce (optional)
2   tablespoons chopped fresh cilantro leaves
    Salt and freshly-ground black pepper

Directions
1. Avocados are oval shaped fruits with black or green skin and a large seed or pit inside. The rest is creamy, green and delicious! You can tell one is ripe when you can squeeze it and it is firm, but not hard. Have **an adult** cut the avocados in half. Remove the skin and discard it. Remember to keep one of the pits for the top!

Guacamole

2. Mash the avocados with a fork in a medium bowl.

3. Add the lime juice and mix thoroughly.

4. Place the onion into a non-metallic sieve or colander, and sprinkle with the salt. Let it stand for 10 minutes.

5. Pour boiling water over the onions and rinse well. Pat dry with paper towels.

6. Add the onions, tomatoes, chilies, hot sauce, and fresh cilantro. Mix well.

7. Season to taste with salt and pepper.

8. Keep covered at room temperature until ready to use. Add the saved avocado pit on the top. It, along with the citrus juice, will help prevent your green guacamole from turning brown!

*NOTE: Be sure to wear plastic gloves when you handle hot (jalapeño) peppers. The seeds and pulp on the inside of the peppers can irritate your skin! And never touch your eyes or face with the gloves after you have touched the pepper seeds.

El Desierto
(Desserts)

In Mexico, when it comes time for dessert, most people reach for a piece of fresh fruit from one of the many farmers' markets. On special occasions, when rich desserts are made, cream is rarely used, but sugar is popular. Traditional favorites include crème caramel and milk pudding. As tasty as they are, they are not terribly healthy because of their high sugar content.

Here are a few Mexican recipes for a sweet treat that are still good for you. Which one will you try first?

These desserts can be used to make Mexican bread pudding.

Crunchy Banana Dessert

Ingredients

6   ripe bananas
½   cup packed brown sugar
      juice of 1 lime
3   tablespoons water
½   cup plus 2 tablespoons plain yogurt
¾   cup heavy cream

Ingredients for crunchy topping

¼   cup butter
5   tablespoons fresh bread crumbs
¼   cup packed brown sugar
½   teaspoon ground cinnamon

Directions

1. Peel the bananas and mash with a fork.
2. In a large skillet, combine the mashed bananas with the sugar, lime juice, and water.
3. Cook the mix over medium heat about 5 minutes.
4. Transfer to a large bowl, add the yogurt and mix well.
5. Whip the cream until it forms soft peaks. Gently fold it into the banana mixture. Have a taste. If it is too sweet, add a little more lemon juice.
6. Pour into individual glasses and refrigerate.

To make the topping

1. Melt the butter in a medium skillet over medium-low heat.
2. Add the bread crumbs and cook, stirring frequently, until the crumbs have soaked up most of the butter and are turning a crispy golden brown.

Banana dessert
with crumbled
bits of bread

3. Add the brown sugar and cinnamon. Stir until the crumbs are coated. Then put on a plate to cool.
4. Just before serving, sprinkle the banana cream with the bread crumb mixture and serve at room temperature.

Mexican Bread Pudding

Bread pudding, a real treat in Mexico, is often terribly rich. In this recipe, most of the sugar and cream are replaced with healthier choices, like apple juice and applesauce. The result is a guilt-free, tasty and lighter dessert that is sure to please everyone.

Ingredients

1¼ cup raisins
¾   cup dried prunes, roughly chopped
¼   cup apple juice
14   stale white bread slices (about 11 ounces) cut into 1-inch cubes.
1¼ cup walnuts, coarsely chopped
¾   cup light cream
1½ cup milk
1⅓ cup applesauce
¼   cup granulated sugar
6   tablespoons unsalted butter, melted
3   large eggs, beaten
1   teaspoon ground cinnamon
½   teaspoon ground nutmeg
2   tablespoons packed brown sugar

Directions

1. Combine the raisins and prunes in a bowl. Set aside to soak for one hour. Then, drain and discard the liquid.
2. Have **an adult** preheat the oven 350° F.
3. Generously butter an 11 x 7 ½-inch baking dish. Scatter the drained raisins and prunes onto the bottom. Cover with the walnuts and stale bread pieces (bread that has been allowed to sit out and become hard and crusty).

Mexican bread pudding

4. Place the cream, milk, apple juice, applesauce, granulated sugar, melted butter, eggs, cinnamon, and nutmeg into a large bowl and mix well.
5. Strain the egg mixture over the bread and cover the dish with foil.
6. Bake until the center of the pudding is set, about one hour.
7. When ready to serve, sprinkle the brown sugar evenly over the pudding and broil for two to three minutes only.

Apple Sauce

Apple sauce is a very popular fruit-based desert. It can be added to other recipes to help replace cream and sugar, or it can be eaten alone. Many Mexicans enjoy adding this applesauce to yogurt or ice cream.

Ingredients

1   pound cooking apples (McIntosh and Granny Smith work well)
    finely grated zest of one lime (zest is finely grated lime skin)
½   teaspoon ground allspice
3   tablespoons water
2   teaspoons sugar
1   tablespoon butter

Directions

1. Have **an adult** peel, quarter, core, and slice the apples.
2. Place the apples in a heavy saucepan with the lime zest, allspice, water, and sugar.
3. Cover and cook over low heat until the apples are soft.
4. Beat in the butter, cool slightly, and add extra sugar, if required.

Applesauce is a wonderful—and tasty—way to help you meet your required daily serving of fruit.

Books

Augustin, Bryon. *The Food of Mexico.* Benchmark Books, 2011.

Barker, Geoff. *Mexico (A World of Food).* Clara House Books, 2010.

Pearce, Kevin. *Foods of Mexico (Culture in the Kitchen).* Gareth Stevens Publishing, 2011.

Wagner, Lisa. *Cool Mexican Cooking: Fun and Tasty Recipes for Kids.* Checkerboard Library, 2011.

Ward, Karen. *Fun with Mexican Cooking.* Powerkids Press, 2009.

Works Consulted

Bayless, Rick. *Authentic Mexican.* New York: W. Morrow, 2007.

Fauchald, Nick. *Funky Chicken Enchiladas and Other Mexican Dishes.* Minnesota: Picture Window Books, 2009.

Kennedy, Diana. *The Art of Mexican Cooking.* New York: Clarkson Porter Publishers, 2008.

Lee, Cecilia Hae-Jin. *Quick & Easy Mexican Cooking.* San Francisco, CA: Chronicle Books, 2011.

On the Internet

DLTK's Crafts for Kids, Mexican Recipes
http://www.dltk-kids.com/world/mexico/recipes.htm

Kid-Friendly Mexican Recipes
http://main.kitchendaily.com/kid-friendly-recipes/mexican/

Mexican Cooking, Kids Cooking Activities
http://www.kids-cooking-activities.com/Mexican-cooking.html

Mexican Made Easy, Cooking with the Kids
http://www.foodnetwork.com/mexican-made-easy/cooking-with-the-kids/index.html

Whale watching off
the coast of Puerto
Vallarta, Mexico.

absorb (ub-ZORB)—Soak up.

appetizer (AA-pih-ty-zer)—A small snack-type food that is served before the main meal.

colander (KAH-lun-der)—A bowl with many small holes that is used for draining water from foods.

colonist (KAH-luh-nist)—A person who moves to another land to live there.

cuisine (kwih-ZEEN)—A type of food from a certain place.

delicioso (dee-lih-see-OH-so)—"Delicious" (in Spanish).

discard (dis-KARD)—Throw away.

disposable (dih-SPOH-zuh-bul)—Able to be thrown away.

hearty (HAR-tee)—Containing plenty of nourishment.

legume (leh-GOOM)—A dry, one-celled fruit that splits naturally down the middle and is usually protected in a pod, such as peas or beans.

originate (or-IH-jih-nayt)—To come from; started.

panini (puh-NEE-nee)—A type of grilled sandwich made with flatbread.

prehistoric (pre-hiss-TOR-ik)—From the time before things were written down or recorded.

preserve—Taking action to keep something in its original state.

savory (SAY-vor-ee)—A flavorful food that is not sweet.

zacahuil (zah-kah-WHEEL)—A huge tamale made in the Huasteca region of Mexico.

Tamra Orr is a fulltime author of over 350 books for young readers of all ages. She is a mother of four and when she isn't writing, she is reading or camping. Orr has a teaching degree from Ball State University and has been writing books for Purple Toad Publishing since they started. Best of all, Orr loves Mexican food and she made sure to taste everything in this book to ensure it was delicious!